Requires Windows 95 or Mac 8.6 or higher

Celebrations and School Events

Creative Clip Art for Classroom and Home
Created and Designed by Dianne J. Hook

ISBN: 1-59441-488-2

Contents

Credits
Illustrator: Dianne J. Hook
Content Design and Project Director: Jennifer Weaver-Spencer
Editor: JulieAnna K. Kirsch
Cover Production: Pam Thayer

Clip Art Assembly Basics

Here are some suggestions to help you make flyers, announcements, or other projects using clip art from this book.

Tools

Putting together the right tools will help your project go more smoothly and look better in the end. A good **copy machine** is a must. It's worth the extra effort to make sure your school or copy shop has machines that make clean copies. You will also need a bottle of white **paper correction fluid**, a fine-tip **black marker** to combine designs and add your own art to the project, **rubber cement** to mount the design onto your paper during the layout stage, and **scissors** for cutting apart the designs you choose. Optional tools to help create a professional-looking project are a **nonreproducible blue pencil**, to make marks that will not show up on copies, a **proportion scale**, to help you determine the size of the reduction or enlargement necessary to fit your paper, and **blue grid paper** for laying out the project with straight lines.

Assembly Steps

1. Choose the design or designs you want to use for your project.

2. Copy the design once from the book so that you have a copy from which to work. This will keep you from having to cut apart your book.

3. Cut out the designs from your copy and lay them out on your paper. (Blue grid paper comes in handy.) A light table can also help with the layout of your page.

4. Next, make a copy of the designs and any text on the paper before adding any other hand-drawn illustrations. Drawing over the grid paper lines is difficult and generally doesn't turn out well.

5. Now you have a good idea of what your project is going to look like. Go ahead and add all the extra finishing touches. Small doodles, simple dots, or squares can really "warm up" the page and keep it from looking choppy.

6. Make final copies of your page.

Hints

- Keep a ¼-inch (0.64 cm) margin on all edges of your paper.
- If the edges of the cutout pieces are visible on your copies, lighten the copy machine one notch or use correction fluid on one copy. Then you can use it to make the final copies.
- Removable tape is great for creating layouts if you will be using the design more than once.

Clip Art Images on CD

Clip art images presented in black and white in this book are available in both black and white and color on the enclosed CD. The CD is Mac and PC compatible and requires an operating system of Windows 95/ Mac 8.6 or higher.

Have fun! You can become an artist and create wonderful projects for your class or home with the help of this book!

Welcome

Open House

Open House

Date: _____

Time: _____

Location: _____

_____

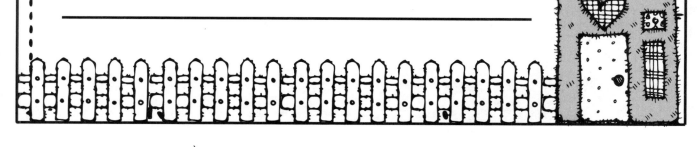

"Come on in!"

The First Day of School

Back to School!

My First
Day of School

Back to
School!

I Love
My School!

13

PTA Meeting

School: _____
Date: _____
Time: _____
Location: _____
_____

PTO Meeting

School: _____
Date: _____
Time: _____
Location: _____
_____

Parent Teacher Conferences

See you there!

Parent Teacher Conference Reminder

Student: _____

Teacher: _____

Date: _____

Time: _____

Location: _____

_____

I'm so Proud!

Wonderful Work!

See you there!

Happy Birthday to You!!!

January	February	March
April	May	June
July	August	September
October	November	December

Wishing You a Happy Birthday!

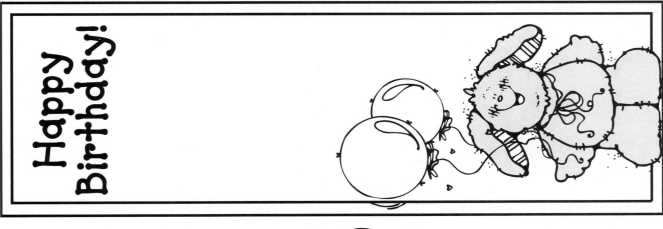

Happy Birthday!

We Missed You !

Get Well Soon!

Field Trip Reminder!

Location:_____

Date:_____

Time:_____

Details:_____

_____

SCHOOL BUS

I'm on a Field Trip!

School:_____

Teacher:_____

We're going on a field trip!

A Special Visitor

Thank You for Visiting!

A Special Visitor
A Classroom Visitor

We Enjoyed
Your Visit!

We Need Volunteers!

We Love Our Volunteers!

Thank You for Volunteering!

To

From

Date

Book Fair!

School: _____

Date: _____

Time: _____

Location: _____

_____

READ!

I ♥ To Read!

Guess Who Lost a Tooth?

I Lost a Tooth!

I Lost a Tooth!

Don't Forget to Brush your Teeth!

It's Time for a Talent Show!

School: _____

Date: _____

Time: _____

Location: _____

_____

Talent Show Participant!

_____
Name

_____
Talent

_____
Date

_____
Signed

Date: _____

Time: _____

SHOW
and
TELL!

Today's
Show and Tell
by:

_____

_____

SHOW
and
TELL!

Author Celebration

_____

_____

_____

_____

_____

Book Celebration

_____

_____

_____

_____

Story Time

Classroom Party!

Date: _____
Time: _____
Location: _____
Details: _____
_____

Let's Celebrate!

January

February

March

April

May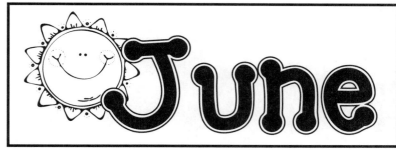

June

July

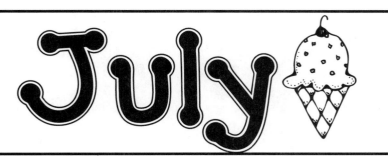

August

36

September

 October

November

December

Fall Festival

Harvest Time

Awesome Autumn

Winter Carnival

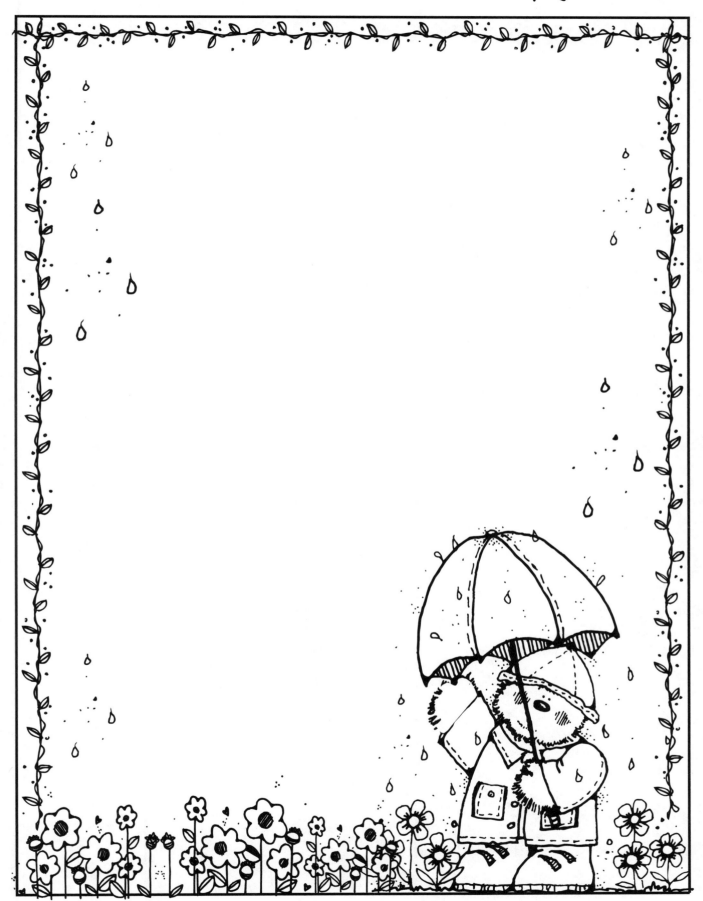

Spring Time Celebration

Don't Forget School Pictures!

School: _____

Date: _____

S M I L E

"Say Cheese!"

Time for a Spelling Bee!

School: _____
Date: _____
Time: _____
Location: _____
_____

Spelling Bee Participant

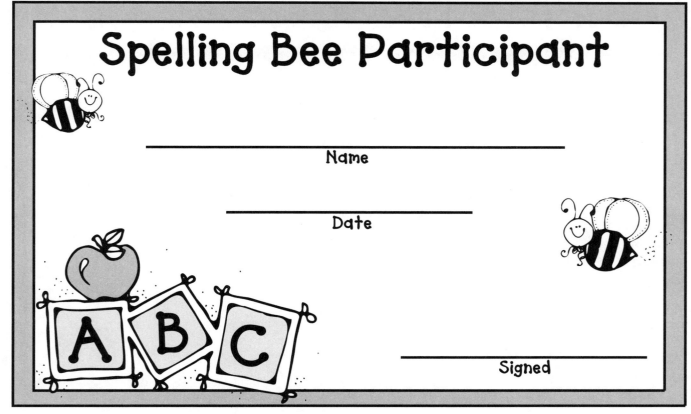

_____
Name

_____
Date

_____
Signed

Science Fair!

School: _____

Date: _____

Time: _____

Location: _____

_____

Science Fair Participant

_____
Name

_____
Project

_____
Date

_____
Signed

Bubble, Bubble... EXPERIMENT!

Field Day!

School: _____
Date: _____
Time: _____
Location: _____
_____

Field Day Participant

_____
Name

_____
Event

_____
Date

_____
Signed

It's Field Day!!!

Field Day Fun!

It's Field Day!!!

Test Time

Test Subject: _____
Date: _____
Time: _____
Location: _____
_____

Quiet Please
Testing in Progress

Super Reader!

_____
Name

_____
Date

_____
Signed

Super Speller!

_____
Name

_____
Date

_____
Signed

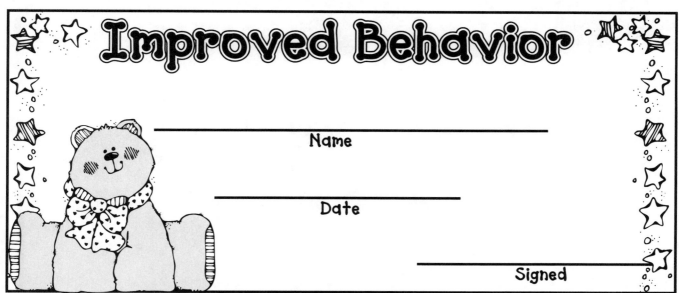

Improved Behavior

_____
Name

_____
Date

_____
Signed

Good Citizen

_____
Name

_____
Date

_____
Signed

Good Sport

_____
Name

_____
Date

_____
Signed

Math Award

_____
Name

_____
Date

_____
Signed

Good Work

Name

Date

Signed

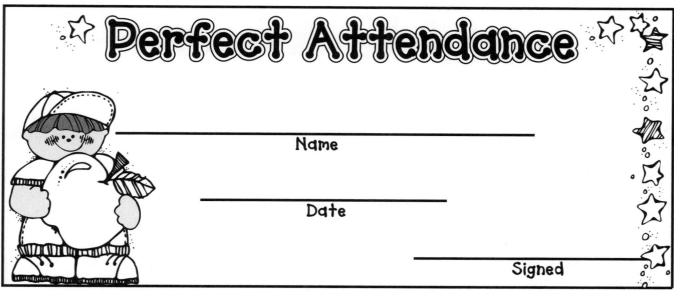

Perfect Attendance

Name

Date

Signed

Good Friend

Name

Date

Signed

Award

_____
Name

_____
Award

_____
Date

_____
Signed

Grrreat Work!

Go For It!
Winner !

Star Student

Hard Worker

Good Citizen

Super Student

School's Out!

SUMMER

Summer Fun!

Summer Reading

Have a Great Summer!

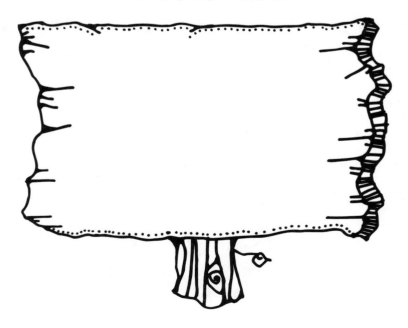

Graduation Announcement

Student: _____
Date: _____
Time: _____
Location: _____
_____

Graduation

Graduation Diploma

_____
Name

_____
Grade

_____
Date

_____
Signed

I Graduated Today!

I Got a Diploma!

100border

 100days

 100pencil

 100topper

 apple

 appleblocks

applebooks

 applerow

 april

 attendance

 august

 award

 balloon1

balloon2

 banner

 bdaybears

 bdaybunny

 bdaychart

 bearapple

 bearbuddies

 bearflag

 bearsign

 beartooth

 bearumbrella

 bee

 bookblocks

 bookopen

 boy1

 boypicture

 bug

 bunnyhearts

 bunnywelcome

 butterfly1

 butterfly2

 camera

 classparty

 clown1

 clown2

 confetti

 cupcake

 december

 doghappy

 dogthankyou

 duck

 february

 fence

 fieldday1

 fieldday2

 fieldday3

 fieldday6

 fieldday6

 fieldtrip

 firstday

 flowers1

 flowers2

 flowers3

 fundraiser

 getwell

 girlbooks

 girlpicture

 goodfriend

 goodwork

 gradannounc...

 gradbear2

 gradcertificate

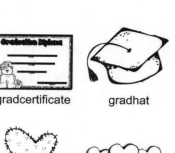 gradhat

 gradsquirrel1

 gradsquirrel2

 graduation

 grass

 haystack

 heartquilt

hearts

hipposign

holly

housequilt

houserow

icecream

 improved

 january

 july

 june

 kidborder

 kidrow

kids

 kites

 leaf

 leafborder

lighbulb

lovetoread

 march

 mathaward

 may

 missedyou

 mousebooks

 mousestar

 november

 october

 openhouse1

 openhouse2

 pandainvite

 parentteacher

 partybears

 pencil

pencilholder

pencilrow

 pumpkinrow

 reader

 ribbon

 scarecrow1

 schoolbus

 schoolhouse

 schoolpics

 sciencefair1

 sciencefair2

 scroll

 september

 shades

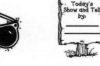 showsign

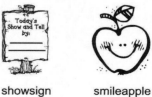 smileapple

 snowbuild

 snowflakes1

 snowflakes2

 snowman

 snowtree

 spellbee

 speller

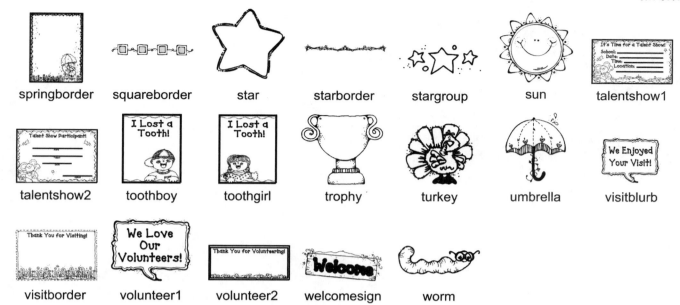

springborder   squareborder   star   starborder   stargroup   sun   talentshow1

talentshow2   toothboy   toothgirl   trophy   turkey   umbrella   visitblurb

visitborder   volunteer1   volunteer2   welcomesign   worm

Please note that all the images in this book are not contained on the CD.

Clip Art Information: DJ Inkers Cut & Copy for Computer CDs contain clip art in both black and white and color. The clip art is NOT a program. It is a collection of art images to be used in a host program. The Windows CDs are formatted with .wmf file types. Macintosh CDs are formatted with .eps and .tiff file types. A host program that supports these file types is required. Recommended host programs for Windows include Print Shop, Print Master, or MS Publisher. Recommended programs for Macintosh include Appleworks or Claris.

Inserting Clip Art into a Host Program: Open a blank document. Click on *Insert > Clip Art > From File*, and select your "c:" drive. Double-click on the DJ Inkers folder, and double-click on the appropriate CD folder (ex. Kidillywinks). Double-click on *Vector*. You will now be able to view all the different images. Click on an image, and select *Insert*. This will insert the image into your document. These instructions can be applied to different host programs, although there may be some variation in the words used. For example, it may say *Import* or *Add* instead of *Insert*.

For further instructions or information, please visit our website, www.djinkers.com. Go to the *Tips & Ideas* section, and click on the *Frequently Asked Questions* link.